THE ANCIENT WORLD

ANCIENT INCAS

BY MICHAEL BURGAN

CHILDREN'S PRESS®
AN IMPRINT OF SCHOLASTIC INC.
NEW YORK   TORONTO   LONDON   AUCKLAND   SYDNEY
MEXICO CITY   NEW DELHI   HONG KONG
DANBURY, CONNECTICUT

Content Consultant
Tamara L. Bray, PhD,
Professor of Anthropology,
Wayne State University,
Detroit, Michigan

Library of Congress Cataloging-in-Publication Data
Burgan, Michael.
  Ancient Incas/by Michael Burgan.
    p. cm.—(The ancient world)
  Includes bibliographical references and index.
  ISBN: 978-0-531-25179-9 (lib. bdg.) — ISBN: 978-0-531-25979-5 (pbk.)
  1. Incas—History—Juvenile literature. 2. Incas—Social life and
customs—Juvenile literature. I. Title.
  F3429.B8493 2012
  985'.01—dc23   2012002159

Photographs © 2013: age fotostock: 89 bottom (ARCO/P. Henry), cover inset right, 1 (Sharron Schiefelbein); Alamy Images: 62 bottom (Edd Westmacott), 38, 62 top (James Brunker), 54 (John Elk III), 13 (Mireille Vautier), 28 (Peter Adams Photography Ltd.), 52 (Susan E. Degginger), 48 bottom (TH Foto); AP Images: 11, 51, 100 top (Martin Mejia), 29, 30, 78, 83 (North Wind Picture Archives); Bridgeman Art Library: 58 (Alberto Salinas (1932-2004)/Private Collection/© Look and Learn), 9 (James Edwin McConnell (1903-95)/Private Collection/© Look and Learn), 92 (Paul Maeyaert), 63, 70 (Private Collection), 66 (Theodore de Bry (1528-98) (after)/Private Collection/The Stapleton Collection); Dreamstime: 96 (Antonella865), 97 (Velvetweb), page borders throughout (Chaosmaker); Getty Images: 95 (Cris Bouroncle/AFP), 68 (Cuan Hansen), 8 (Danita Delimont), 90 (Dorling Kindersley); iStockphoto/The Power of Forever Photography: 20, 103 top; Media Bakery: 49; National Geographic Stock: 82 (David Evans), 46, 89 top (H.M. Herget), 16 (Kenneth Garrett), 36, 74 (Maria Stenzel), 24 (Ned M. Seidler); North Wind Picture Archives: 12 top, 31, 87, 88, 91, 102 top; Shutterstock, Inc.: cover main (Alfredo Cerra), 37 (Carlos E. Santa Maria), 48 top (Dmitrijs Bindemanis), 26 (James Harrison), 76 bottom (Jo Mikus), 47 (kastianz), 19, 103 bottom (Mark Skalny), 81 (Rafal Cichawa), 6 (tr3gin); Superstock, Inc.: 85 (age fotostock), 76 top (Eye Ubiquitous), 55 (Gerard Lacz Images), 57 (John Warburton Lee), 25, 27, 101 top (Pantheon), 12 bottom, 71 (Robert Harding Picture Library); The Granger Collection: 34 top, 40, 43, 44, 56, 61, 72, 75, 93 (Felipe Guaman Poma de Ayala.), back cover top, cover inset left, 3, 23, 32, 77; The Image Works: 65 (AAAC/TopFoto), 4, 59, 67 (akg-images/Bildarchiv Steffens), 60 (akg-images/Werner Forman), 86, 102 bottom (J. Bedmar/Iberfoto), 15, 17, 73, 100 bottom (Mary Evans Picture Library), 10, 101 bottom (Michael Mirecki/Impact/HIP), 14 (Mireille Vautier/akg-images), 21 (P. Rotger/Iberfoto), 34 bottom (Patricio Crooker/fotosbolivia), 7 (Robert Gibbs/Impact/HIP), 5, 33, 39, 53, 80, 84 (Werner Forman/TopFoto).

Maps by XNR Productions, Inc.

1 2 3 4 5 6 7 8 9 10 R 22 21 20 19 18 17 16 15 14 13

JOURNEY BACK TO THE ANCIENT INCAS

The Incas left behind no written records of their history.

Millions of people still speak the ancient language of the Inca empire today.

The Incas constructed many of their buildings out of carefully cut stones that fit precisely together.

TABLE OF CONTENTS

A ceremonial
drinking vessel

The Past Is Present

See for yourself how the ancient Inca culture is still present in our lives today.

An Inca ceramic statue

UP IN THE MOUNTAINS

In the Andes of South America, among some of the world's tallest mountains, different cultures rose and fell. Over a span of several thousand years, people learned to grow crops at high altitudes, create beautiful objects out of silver and gold, and

Sites such as Llactapata have provided scholars with valuable information about the Inca.

construct massive buildings of stone. The last and greatest of the
Andean civilizations was the Incas.

Starting from their high-altitude homeland of Cuzco, in what
is now Peru, the Incas created a massive empire in the **Western
Hemisphere**. They took little over a century to spread their
control over a slice of land that stretched 2,400 miles (3,862 kilometers) from north to south. The western border was the Pacific
Ocean, and to the east were the jungles of the Amazon rain forest.
In this long, narrow empire, the Incas and the people they conquered lived within a variety of climates and landforms.

*The Inca built their
civilization among the
highlands of the Andes
Mountains.*

**Western
Hemisphere** (WES-
turn HEM-i-sfeer) the
half of the world that
includes North and
South America and the
waters around these
two continents

The Incas were certainly conquerors, with all young males receiving military training. But they were also great builders whose precise stonework and network of highways continue to impress modern engineers. The Incas were skilled artists and mathematicians, too. Because they were smart rulers, the Incas were able to successfully build and run an empire. The Incas moved people across the empire to suit their purposes. People who might rebel were sent to live among more loyal citizens. In turn, trusted communities were moved to newly defeated regions, to help introduce Inca rule. The Incas also set up an economic system that generated surplus and allowed the state to provide food to the people for special celebrations and during times of **famine**.

The Inca emperor was not merely a head of state. To the people of the Empire, he was also a god, and religion played a key role in daily life. The Incas worshipped several deities as well as sacred places on the landscape, and their religious beliefs were shaped by the Andean civilizations that came before them. Elements of the Inca belief system live on today in remote areas of Peru and Bolivia.

Inca craftsmen carved axe heads and other tools from a variety of materials.

famine (FAM-in) a serious lack of food in a geographic area

Where those ancient beliefs continue to exist, they are mixed with the Christianity introduced by the Spanish **conquistadores**. During the 1500s, Spain sent these explorers and soldiers around the world to claim new lands for the kingdom. They sought wealth and to spread their Roman Catholic religion. The Spanish who came to Inca lands saw the gold and other valuables there, and quickly seized control. From then on, the Andean world was shaped by European influences.

Although the Inca Empire was defeated by the Spaniards, elements of ancient Andean practices live on today, and the Incas' accomplishments still fascinate people around the world.

conquistadores
(kahn-KEES-tuh-dohrz)
soldiers sent to seize
foreign lands for Spain

The Spanish used force to take control of the Inca Empire.

CHAPTER ONE

A RAPID RISE TO POWER

T he Cuzco valley was the homeland of the Inca. This valley is situated some 10,000 feet (3,048 meters) above sea level in what is now south-central Peru. It is surrounded by the high peaks of the Andes mountains. More than one thousand years ago, this valley was inhabited by a number of different ethnic groups, among them were the Inca. For several centuries,

Some Inca ruins still stand in the Cuzco valley.

these different ethnic groups jostled with one another for power. At some point, the Inca defeated all their neighbors in the Cuzco valley and then set out to conquer others in more distant areas.

The early history of the Incas is cloaked in mystery, as they left no written records. Modern historians rely on **archaeology** for some of their knowledge of the first Incas. Other information comes from the books written by the Spanish who first conquered the Inca Empire and other Spaniards who followed. Several generations later, a few native people educated by the Spanish also wrote down what they remembered about the Inca Empire.

Archaeological discoveries have helped shed light on the history of the Incas.

archaeology (ar-kee-AH-luh-jee) the study of the distant past, which often involves digging up old buildings, objects, and bones and examining them carefully

The Past Is Present
FLOATING STONES

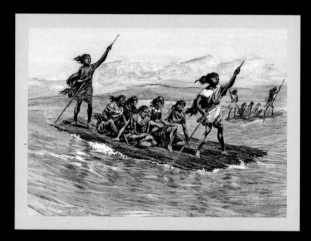

Along Lake Titicaca, people used the *totora* reed to build boats, both before and during Inca rule. They tied together bundles of the reeds, which then could carry people and goods on the water. In 2002, archaeologists recruited some local boatbuilders to test a theory: that the Tiwanaku, who were predecessors of the Incas, used reed boats to move huge building stones across the lake. The archaeologists used almost 1.8 million reeds to construct a boat about 45 feet (14 m) long. They used it to move a 9-ton stone across Lake Titicaca. The experiment showed that technology available more than a thousand years ago would have let Andean people use their simple reed boats to move massive loads. Because the reeds are plentiful and grow locally, totora reed boats are still used today on the waters of Lake Titicaca in Peru and Bolivia.

Two Myths

Archaeological evidence suggests that the Incas arrived in the Cuzco valley around 1200 CE. The Incas had stories of their own that explained who they were, where they came from, and how they began to build an empire. In one story, four brothers and four sisters were said to have emerged from a cave called Tampu T'uqu, south of Cuzco. According to the myth, these eight people were the first Incas. They led others from the region to find land where they could raise crops, telling the people they met that they were children of the god Wiraqocha, the creator of the universe.

During their journey, two of the brothers turned to stone. The others finally reached a spot that seemed suitable for growing crops and declared it their new home. This was the Cuzco basin. Because it was already occupied, the Inca had to defeat the people living there. Following their victory, another of the brothers turned to stone and became a famous landmark on a hill above Cuzco. The remaining brother, Manco Qhapaq, became the first Inca king.

According to legend, Manco Qhapaq was the founder of the Inca Empire.

Mama Ocllo is a key figure in some versions of the Inca origin myth.

Another version of the Inca origin myth focuses on Manco Qhapaq and his sister Mama Ocllo. They were said to have been created by the sun god Inti. The two siblings lived on an island in Lake Titicaca, in what is now Bolivia. Inti sent them out to spread culture to all the people of the world. Manco Qhapaq had a golden stick that he used to test the ground as he traveled. Reaching Cuzco, the stick sunk into the ground, meaning he and his followers should settle there. In both tales, the Incas expressed a belief that they had been chosen by the gods to rule over other people.

Another key historical myth explains the rise of the great Inca Empire. Their eighth king, named for the god Wiraqocha, faced a threat from the ethnic group known as the Chankas. This group lived west of Cuzco, and they demanded that Wiraqocha surrender to them. Instead, he left the city. His son Inca Yupanqui, however, wanted to fight, but could not amass an army from the people in and around Cuzco. In a dream, a god appeared and told him he would be a great Inca leader. Then, stones in the field outside Cuzco magically came to life as warriors. Inca Yupanqui led these warriors to victory against the Chankas. He became the king of the Incas, having earned the new name of Pachakuti—"transformer of the world."

Pachakuti's stone warriors were a myth, but historians accept that he was a real Inca leader and one who helped create the Inca Empire. A battle with the Chankas probably did take place, as they were a real people near Cuzco.

Pachakuti is one of the earliest Inca leaders whose existence can be confirmed.

INFLUENCES ON THE INCAS

The Incas were not the first people in the Andes to create an empire. Many centuries prior, another highland people known as the Wari established control over a vast portion of the Andes. The homeland of the Wari was located hundreds of miles to the northwest of the Cuzco valley. Beginning around 600 CE, the Wari began to spread outward from their home territory, conquering other ethnic groups and setting up colonies. Wari traders brought goods from far away. The Wari built a road system to link their colonies, which the Incas later used and expanded. Many archaeologists think Wari art and government also influenced the Incas.

At about the same time that the Wari were expanding their empire from the central highlands of Peru, the Tiwanaku were

Archaeologists have discovered a variety of Wari ruins, artifacts, and tombs in Peru.

building their own empire from their homeland on the southern shores of Lake Titicaca in modern-day Bolivia. The Tiwanaku also ruled a small empire that spread its influence into the Cuzco valley. Like the Wari, the Tiwanaku set up small colonies far from the central city, controlling land that stretched from the highlands around the Andes down to the Pacific coast. The Incas seem to have borrowed some ideas on religion and architecture from the Tiwanaku.

This modern illustration imagines what Mayta Qhapaq may have looked like.

WARRING TIMES

By about 1000 or 1100, both the Wari and Tiwanaku empires had collapsed. With these influences gone in the Cuzco valley, the different local ethnic groups that lived there began to compete for power. The Incas were one of these groups. By the end of the 1200s, the Incas were asserting themselves in the valley. They continued to extend their influence through marriage with the leaders of other communities and through war. Inca accounts indicate that their fourth king, Mayta Qhapaq, spread Inca rule through a large part of the Cuzco valley. In the past, the Incas might have raided an enemy only to seize goods they wanted. After Mayta Qhapaq, they sought to conquer and control their enemies.

Once they had political control, the Incas took goods from their defeated foes, then made them pay **tribute** in the form of labor. Defeated people had to perform work for the Sapa Inca—the "unique Inca," the title of the Inca king. Using this labor, the kings built palaces and government buildings, roads, fortresses, and other monumental works. All people conquered by the Inca provided labor of some kind to the Inca state instead of paying taxes in goods. Military service was another form of this work.

But the Incas also believed in the idea of **reciprocity**. While the people they ruled worked for them, the Incas gave them the materials they needed to perform their duties, as well as food and clothing. At other times, the Inca held large celebrations as a way of thanking the people for their labor. At these parties, the Inca provided the people with food and a special kind of fermented beverage called *chicha,* made from corn. The rulers were also responsible for carrying out religious ceremonies thought to benefit the whole society. Reciprocity was a key element of Andean life.

MILITARY POWER

Major expansion of the Inca Empire began under the reign of the ninth king, Pachakuti, who conquered lands both north and south of Cuzco. Under his rule, the Inca took control of land on the western side of Lake Titicaca.

According to Inca histories, Pachakuti oversaw the construction of many buildings during the times when he was not fighting. Cuzco was completely remade as Pachakuti moved everyone out of the city and erected new buildings. Some archaeologists doubt

Machu Picchu was built as a royal estate during the reign of Pachakuti.

this happened, since walls from before the rise of the Incas have been found in modern Cuzco. But no one doubts that the Incas carefully planned the streets and grand buildings that filled their capital.

Pachakuti also built several estates—palaces and surrounding farmlands where he and members of his royal family went to rest in a beautiful, peaceful spot. Of all the Incan royal estates, the most famous is Machu Picchu. The Spanish never found the site, so it was considered a lost city until the archaeologist Hiram Bingham

A surprising number of buildings remain mostly intact at the ruins of Machu Picchu.

CVSCO. REGNI PERV IN NOVO ORBE CAPVT.

Inca leaders sometimes met with foreign leaders at Cuzco in attempts to avoid unnecessary battles.

came upon it in 1911. But several Europeans knew about Machu Picchu before Bingham, as did local Peruvians. The site is famous for its impressive stonework and the way the buildings blend into the mountainside. Machu Picchu could house up to 750 people, and archaeologists once thought it was a fort, but recent studies suggest its role as an estate. A popular tourist attraction, Machu Picchu is one of the greatest surviving links to the Incas.

subjects (SUHB-jekts) people who live under the authority of a king or queen

As the Incas gained control of a larger region, they sometimes had to send their armies back to lands they had already conquered. This was because the local people sometimes tried to rebel against foreign rule, especially when a new Inca king came to power. To limit rebellions and ensure loyalty, the Inca created a class of people called *mitmaq*. These were people forced to move from their homelands to other parts of the empire. The Incas placed the defeated mitmaq in areas where there were many loyal **subjects**. They then moved other loyal tribes into the now-empty area, so they could work the defeated enemies' fields. Mitmaq could also be moved for purely economic reasons, such as to begin farming new lands in different parts of the empire.

All-out war was not the Incas' first choice for gaining new lands and tribute. At times, they sent messages to distant cities, inviting leaders or diplomats to come to Cuzco. The aim was to force the city to accept Inca rule without a fight. If the invited leaders did not respond—or, as in some cases, if they mistreated the Inca messengers—then the Sapa Inca sent a large army to the offending city. Just seeing such Inca military often convinced the enemies to surrender.

When actual battles took place, the Inca army used its superb organizational skills and overwhelming size to defeat its foes. Weapons included clubs, spears, knives, and slingshots. People from the Amazon region who were drafted into the Inca army used bows and arrows. Andean peoples also used a throwing weapon called a bola. It had several weights made of metal or stone attached to separate strings, which were tied together. The Incas used bolas to trip up enemy soldiers so they could kill them with clubs. Bolas are still sometimes used in South America to catch runaway animals. For defense, the Incas used shields and wore heavy cotton armor.

The largest division in the Inca army had ten thousand men, and a single army could have three or more divisions. The divisions were broken down into smaller units, and men from the same regions fought together. The king also had his own specially trained force of five thousand men to protect him during military **campaigns**.

campaigns (kam-PAYNZ) organized actions in order to achieve a particular goal

This Peruvian artwork depicts Inca warriors overpowering their foes.

In a typical battle, the two sides first launched rocks, spears, and arrows at each other. Then the opposing warriors rushed across the battlefield to fight in hand-to-hand combat. The goal was to kill as many soldiers as quickly as possible, so the enemy would retreat. The size of the Inca army helped make this easier. The Incas also used several tactics to make the enemy do what they wanted. At times, the Incas pretended to retreat so the enemy would chase them to a spot where the Incas had a better chance of winning. Other times, they set fires to force the enemy to move.

Road systems made it easy for the Incas to move huge armies throughout their territory.

Inca king Topa Inca Yupanqui extended Inca influence south into what is now central Chile.

Feeding and supplying such a large army far from Cuzco was demanding, but the Inca road system made it easier. So did the storehouses built along major highways. Called *qolkas*, these buildings were filled with weapons, clothing, and food. Qolkas were often associated with a *tambo*, which was an Inca site located along the royal road that had rooms where government officials could stay as they traveled about the empire. Tambos were located about 12 miles (19 km) apart from one another.

This Chimú statue was uncovered in the ruins of Chan Chan, in modern-day Peru.

mummy (MUHM-ee) a dead body that has been preserved with special chemicals and wrapped in cloth

A GROWING EMPIRE

In Inca society, land and wealth did not pass from a king to his successor when he died. In fact, the new king did not inherit anything when he took power. But he was expected to provide food, housing, and shelter for his extended family. So each new king needed to conquer lands that would be a source of wealth for his relatives. When a king died, his lands provided for his remaining relatives and covered the costs of preserving and caring for his **mummy**. Since early kings had taken all the land near Cuzco, later ones had to go farther in search of new lands.

The impressive military conquests that began under Pachakuti continued under the next king, Topa (or Tupac) Inca Yupanqui, the son of Pachakuti. His conquests extended the empire north into modern-day Ecuador and south into what are now Argentina and Chile. Under Topa Inca, the Incas gained more land than they ever had before.

With these gains, for the first time the Incas had control over peoples along the Pacific coast. These peoples included the Chimú, who had previously ruled their own empire from their capital of Chan Chan. With their own great wealth, the Chimú were important rivals to the Incas' power. Once he defeated the Chimú, Topa Inca took their silver and gold, and sent their skilled **artisans** to Cuzco and other Inca cities. Not trusting the loyalty of the Chimú, the king never let them keep weapons or serve in the army as other defeated peoples did.

Like earlier kings, Topa Inca tried to win the support of some people by both offering gifts and threatening all-out warfare. The people of Huarco, though, resisted Inca rule for several years. Their land was close to the Pacific Ocean, west of Cuzco. To conquer Huarco, Topa Inca built a new city, called Inkawasi, to serve as a military base.

artisans (AHR-ti-zuhnz) people who are skilled at working with their hands at a particular craft

Wayna Qhapaq struggled with his brothers for the position of Sapa Inca after the death of Topa Inca.

LAST CONQUESTS

Topa Inca's son Wayna Qhapaq became the eleventh Sapa Inca. He conquered some parts of the eastern foothills of the Andes mountains in Peru and Ecuador, and extended the empire northward to the border of modern-day Colombia. Wayna Qhapaq was born in Tumibamba, an imperial city in southern Ecuador that had become a base for Inca operations

in the region. Today, the modern city of Cuenca sits atop the ruins of Tumibamba. Under Wayna Qhapaq, the city served almost as a second capital, though it was more than 1,000 miles (1,609 km) from Cuzco. That great distance made it hard for him to stay in contact with nobles and government officials back in Cuzco.

Cuenca, Ecuador, is located on the same land where Wayna Qhapaq's hometown once stood.

Wayna Qhapaq's armies in Ecuador endured fierce fighting as they tried to move northward. One people, the Cañari, were particularly hard to defeat, and the Incas suffered high losses battling them. By some accounts, many of the Cañari became mitmaq, to reduce the chance of further rebellion in the region.

Although Wayna Qhapaq succeeded in subduing the local ethnic groups in northern Ecuador after many years of fighting, Inca control over these groups was not strong.

Around 1525, the Inca king received reports of strange men with light skin and beards reaching Inca lands. Before he could react to the news and what it might mean, the king fell ill from a disease. The illness was mysterious to the Incas, since they had never seen it before. They did not know that the strangers and the disease were linked.

The arrival of the Spanish marked the beginning of the end of the Inca Empire.

The Spanish brought the deadly disease smallpox with them when they arrived in America.

The foreigners were Spanish soldiers. The disease was most likely smallpox, which the conquistadores had brought from Europe. It and other European diseases spread into the Inca Empire, killing hundreds of thousands of people. Smallpox also killed Wayna Qhapaq's young son Ninan Cuyochi. The king had wanted Ninan Cuyochi to be the next Sapa Inca, but now two of his other sons fought for control of the empire.

CIVIL WAR

When Wayna Qhapaq had marched north to conquer the hostile peoples living around the equator, he had left his son Waskar in charge of Cuzco. Waskar expected to be the next king, and nobles in Cuzco supported his claim to the throne. In Quito, though, generals who had fought with Wayna Qhapaq supported Atawallpa, who had helped his father during the northern campaigns. Atawallpa claimed that he should rule the entire empire, and the two brothers began a civil war. The fighting lasted until 1532, and saw the death of thousands of warriors and the destruction of grand cities such as Tumibamba. In the end, Atawallpa's forces captured and killed Waskar and took Cuzco. But before Atawallpa could take the throne, the Spanish once again made their presence known. The Inca Empire was about to crumble.

The Spanish approached the Inca toward the end of the empire's civil war.

CHAPTER TWO

KEEPING ORDER

A group of men walked forward in two parallel lines, sharing the weight of two long poles placed across their shoulders. The poles held a **litter** covered with gold, rare

Men carried the Sapa Inca in a litter so he would not have to walk.

The Inca created many beautiful decorations using gold and feathers

feathers, and precious gems. Inside sat the Sapa Inca, traveling to the city center to speak to his people. In wartime, he would ride in an open litter, so he could command his troops.

By any title—king, emperor, Sapa Inca—the man who ruled the Incas controlled great wealth and military power. To the Incas, he was the son of their sun god, and so a god himself. He wore the finest clothes and decorated himself with gold. But to use his great power over such a large empire, an Inca king relied on the skills of many government officials. At times, he had to react to the desires of others—including rebellious defeated kings, relatives, and religious **oracles**—rather than merely do what he wanted.

litter (LIT-ur) a covered couch or seat that is carried by several people

oracles (OR-uh-kulz) people who are thought to be in touch with gods and spirits and can predict the future; also, the places where those people deliver their messages from the gods

MOUNTAINTOP FARMING

The Incas were not the only ancient people to use terraces for farming, but they were experts at building them. Houses were also built on terraces. To create basic terraces, the Incas dug into the side of a mountain to create a flat area, then built a stone wall to hold back the exposed earth. To make the terrace suitable for growing crops, they first put down a layer of small rocks. Then they added smaller rocks and sand, and finally a layer of soil that they had carried up

from other areas, such as river bottoms. The different layers kept the ground well drained, so water didn't collect on the surface. The stone walls helped keep the crops warm during colder weather. The sun heated the stones during the day, and the stones released that heat over the crops at night, when temperatures fell. Some of the terraces the Incas built, along with canals that brought water to them, are still used for farming today.

THE LIFE OF A KING

A ruling Sapa Inca sometimes chose the son who would follow him. Other times, male members of the royal family made this decision. The king-to-be was expected to show his skills as a great warrior. With the Sapa Inca's death, he stepped up to the throne. Topa Inca was said to have started the tradition of the king marrying his primary wife—his sister—at the same time he became king. The **coronation** of a king was both a religious event and a great feast. Humans and animals were **sacrificed** to the gods, and great nobles from across the empire traveled to Cuzco for the ceremonies.

Once in power, the Sapa Inca had several duties. He served as the commander of the military and oversaw the many festivals that took place. When he spoke to crowds, he did so from atop an *ushnu*, a stepped stone platform that rose above the plaza. These platforms were built in the centers of important settlements across the empire. In his palace, the king sometimes sat behind a screen so his guests could not see him. Aides gave his messages to guests, so he did not have to speak directly to them. Under Inca law, people coming to meet the king had to take off their shoes and carry something heavy on their backs. All these measures were meant to show how special, how godlike, the king was compared to everyone else. Yet the king was still human, and he relied on his relatives and close nobles to advise him. A king could also be the target of murder by family members who opposed his rule.

The king was not only the head of state. He was also in charge of a family group called a *panaca*. The lands that each king conquered for himself were supposed to support the panaca both during and after his life. The members of the panaca took care of the king's mummy after his death. A dead king's living relatives treated his

coronation (kor-uh-NAY-shun) the ceremony in which a king, queen, or other ruler is crowned

sacrificed (SAK-ruh-fyst) killed as an offering to a god

mummy as if it were still a member of the family. The panaca offered the mummy food, put it to bed, and took it out for special feasts. Some relatives were believed to be able to communicate with mummies and express their thoughts.

Inca kings used the labor of conquered people for many massive building projects. These included the construction of stone aqueducts, which carried water from distant springs and rivers to cities. They also included large, stone-faced terraces. The terraces, built into mountainsides, helped increase the land available for Incas to farm. The kings also built a road system, the Qhapaq Nan. One main route ran from Cuzco to Quito. Two other roads ran south

Mummies were often bundled with various household objects.

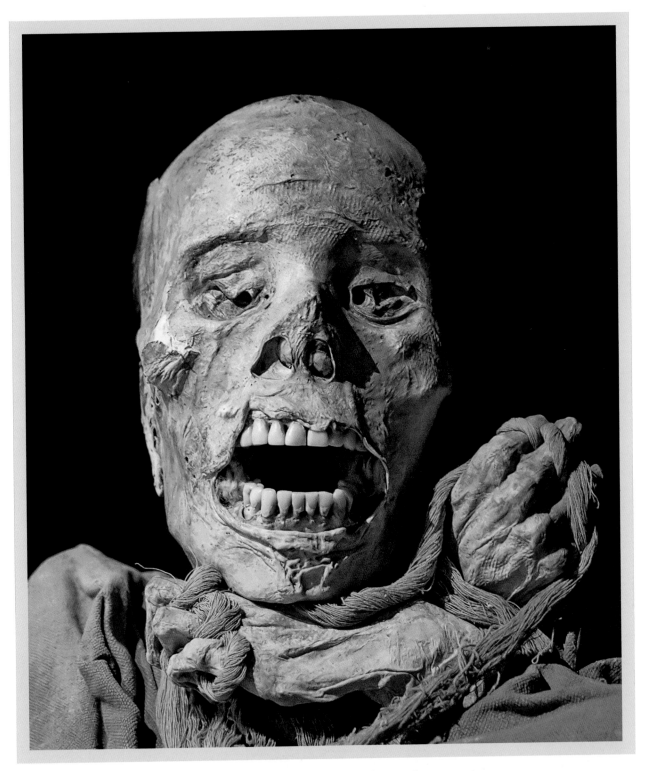

Archaeologists have discovered thousands of ancient Inca mummies.

from the capital into Chile and Argentina. Countless other roads branched off from the main routes. The main highways were for royal use only. Common people needed permission to use them.

Today, the Qhapaq Nan passes through six different countries.

THE ORGANIZATION OF THE EMPIRE

The Incas called their empire Tawantinsuyu. The name means "four parts together," because the Incas divided their land into four sections, or *suyus*. The capital city of Cuzco was the geographic center of the four parts. Going clockwise from north to south, the four suyus were Chinchaysuyu, Antisuyu, Qollasuyu, and Kuntisuyu. The first two suyus were considered the upper half of the empire and the second two were the lower. By the time of the Spanish conquest, Chinchaysuyu was the most important division, as it had more people and greater wealth than the other three combined.

Each suyu had a leader called an *apo*. These officials were usually relatives of the king and served as his top advisers. Within each suyu were provinces. The empire had about 80 provinces in all. The Incas tried to arrange the provinces so that people from the same ethnic groups lived together. Each province had a governor who reported to the apo of his division. The governors were usually ethnic Incas. This means they were descended from original Incas as opposed to members of a defeated people.

Important officials called *khipukamayuqs* helped the governors run the provinces. Their name came from the main tool of their trade, a series of knotted strings called a *khipu*. A khipu was the Inca record-keeping system, and the khipukamayuqs were similar to accountants. With their khipu, they recorded such things as the amount of tribute received, how much food was stored in a warehouse, and the population of a given area. Messengers carried khipus from the provinces to Cuzco, so the king could keep track of all this information. The messengers, like the khipukamayuqs, were chosen

Despite their simple appearance, khipus could record a wide range of information.

Some of each farmer's livestock products were given to government and religious officials.

by the Inca government. Other government workers included the men in charge of state-owned workshops, the clerks who ran the storehouses, and engineers for huge building projects.

CONTROL AT THE LOCAL LEVEL

Each province had a capital city, which was home to its governor. These cities were religious as well as political centers, and they also held storehouses of food and military supplies. The Incas created provinces that would have room for twenty thousand or thirty thousand households, and each household was required to provide labor to the king. A household could include grandparents, aunts, and uncles, as well as a married couple and their children.

A group of ten thousand households was known as a *saya*, and the person in charge of a saya was called a *kuraka*. A saya kuraka oversaw two lower-ranked kurakas, each of whom was in charge of five thousand households. The system was set up so that each kuraka had lower kurakas under him who were in charge of a smaller number of households, down to a level of just ten households. All but the two lowest levels of kurakas passed their jobs on to their sons. The kurakas' job was to make sure all households provided *mit'a*, or labor, as required and generally obeyed Inca law.

Through expansion, the Incas introduced this system to foreign people who might not want Inca rule. The top kurakas were usually local nobles. The Incas let them stay in power, but expected loyalty in return. One way to ensure this loyalty was to take the kurakas' sons to Cuzco as hostages. A kuraka knew his obedience would affect how the Incas treated his son. While in Cuzco, the sons learned the official language of the empire, called Quechua, and Inca culture.

Although local rulers remained in place in the provinces, the Incas did assert their control. The Sapa Inca claimed all the local lands for himself. The people, though, could keep part of the crops they raised. The rest went to the Incas, divided between the king and the state religion. Llama and alpaca herds and the lands they grazed were also divided this way.

Because reciprocity was part of Andean life, the Inca kings tried to make it part of their governing of the empire. They did not simply take what they wanted from local kurakas—they asked for it. The kurakas agreed, knowing that they faced Inca military might if they refused. The Inca king then gave the people food and entertainment, their part of the reciprocal relationship. This style of government was an attempt to copy the kind of reciprocity that was part of Andean life on the local level. People who came from common **ancestors** helped one another. But the Incas' intentions were false in a way, because the threat of violence was always behind the supposed bonds of reciprocity.

Inca Law

Kurakas played a major role in the Inca **judicial** system by settling disputes between members of their division. If a legal case involved members of different divisions—say two groups of one hundred households—the kuraka at the next highest level heard the case. Inca law dealt with issues such as theft and the rights of different tribes. Lying and laziness were also crimes. According to the seventeenth-century Spanish priest Bernabé Cobo, a person of high social rank usually received a lighter sentence than a commoner did for committing the same crime. The nobles merely faced public scolding for their crimes.

ancestors (AN-ses-turz) relatives who lived long ago

judicial (joo-DISH-uhl) having to do with a court of law or a judge

*Inca landowners sometimes ceremonially cut into the soil as
the workers began planting the land.*

Punishments for criminals were sometimes very harsh.

Many crimes were punishable by whippings. A person caught trying to betray the government was often thrown into a jail cell filled with snakes and vicious animals. Others found guilty of betraying the government had their eyes plucked out. The harshest punishment was death. An Inca who stole from a government field was executed. So were nobles caught having relationships with people who were not their husbands or wives. Cases that could bring the death penalty were heard by governors or the king himself. Kurakas who killed people without approval from higher officials faced public beatings. If a kuraka repeated this crime a second time, he was killed.

Most laws came from old tribal traditions, but the Sapa Inca could create new laws as he saw fit. Whatever their source, Inca laws and the punishments for breaking them helped the Sapa Inca rule over a vast empire.

CHAPTER THREE

FROM THE OCEAN TO THE RAIN FORESTS

Living high in the Andes, the Incas revered the mountain peaks around them as gods or holy beings. Many Incas lived and worked at altitudes more than 2 miles (3 km) above sea level. But their conquests took them into regions that had climates

The Incas built their settlements high up on the mountaintops of the Andes.

and geography much different than those of their homeland. The empire at its peak included some of the land of six modern nations: Colombia, Ecuador, Peru, Bolivia, Chile, and Argentina.

The Andes Mountains stretch over about 5,500 miles (8,851 km).

THE PACIFIC COAST

Scientists have identified 117 different life zones on Earth. Each zone has specific kinds of plants and animals, based on its altitude and distance from the equator. Peru is home to 84 of those zones, which shows just how diverse the Inca lands were.

The Past Is Present

ALL ABOUT QUININE

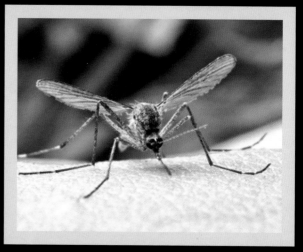

Throughout the Andes, and in many other parts of the world, a deadly disease known as malaria is spread by mosquito bites. The Inca fought the fevers brought on by malaria by taking a medicine that they made by grinding up the bark of the cinchona tree.

Today, scientists know that this remedy works because the cinchona bark contains a chemical called quinine. The chemical gets its name from the Quechua word for the bark of the cinchona tree. Quinine is still used to treat malaria, and its bitter flavor has made it popular as one of the main ingredients in tonic water.

Within the empire were three distinct geographic regions, each with many life zones. Moving from west to east, the first of these regions was the Pacific coast. The Incas controlled about 2,400 miles (3,862 km) of coastline, and the coastal region varied in width from about 60 miles (97 km) in the north to about 12 miles (19 km) in the south.

This region's climate is shaped by the waters of the Pacific Ocean—specifically, a **current** called the Humboldt. Cold waters from Antarctica ride north along this current toward Peru. As offshore winds pass over the cold sea, they are also cooled. Once the winds reach land, they begin to warm, and this increase in temperature keeps any moisture in the air from falling to the ground as

current (KUR-uhnt) the movement of water in a definite direction in a river or an ocean

The Pacific coast is largely a desert in the areas conquered by the Inca.

rain. As a result, most of the coastal region is a desert. Some parts of the coastal desert go years without receiving any rain. But in the winter (which comes during North America's summer), large areas of the coast are blanketed with fog. The moisture in this fog helps some plants live in certain places, but other areas of the desert are too dry to support any plant life. This lack of water also limits where humans can settle on the coast.

In certain years, the weather along the coast changes dramatically. Winds over the Pacific become calm, and the usually cold waters near Peru become warm. With the warm waters comes rain—sometimes enough to create damaging floods. This abnormal weather pattern is now called El Niño, and it affects large parts of the world. The Incas and other Andean people dealt with its effects in different ways.

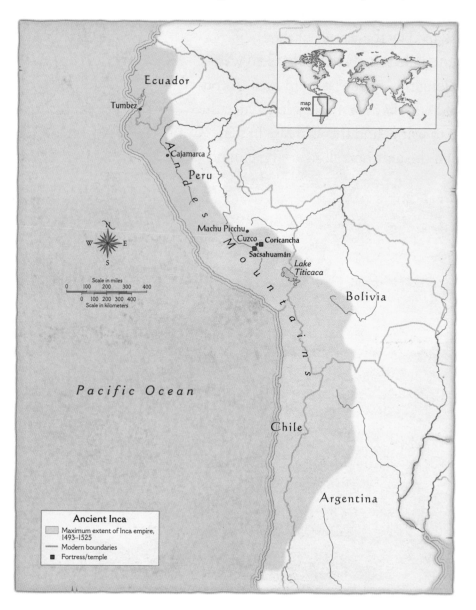

Ecuador

Tumbez

Cajamarca

Peru

Machu Picchu
Cuzco Coricancha
Sacsahuamán

Lake Titicaca

Bolivia

Pacific Ocean

Chile

Argentina

map area

N
W E
S

Scale in miles
0 100 200 300 400
0 100 200 300 400
Scale in kilometers

Ancient Inca
Maximum extent of Inca empire, 1493–1525
Modern boundaries
■ Fortress/temple

El Niño floods have occurred for more than ten thousand years. Some archaeologists believe that the Incas sacrificed people to try to convince the gods to end these heavy rains. Remains found at several Inca temples belonged to sacrifice victims connected to El Niño.

Even today, people living along the coast in South America must contend with destructive El Niño flooding.

Wildlife of the Coastal Region
The cold waters of the Humboldt Current did more than shape the Incas' weather. They also provided a home to tiny sea creatures that served as food for the area's plentiful fish species. In turn, the fish

Spiny oysters were prized by the ancient Inca.

were a food source for sea mammals, such as whales and seals, and seabirds. Sea mammals, fish, and shellfish were a major source of food for the coastal people of the Inca Empire. The waters off the coast of Peru remain some of the world's best fishing grounds.

One shellfish, the spiny oyster, was found only off the coast of Ecuador. The shells of these animals were prized by many Andean peoples. The Incas and others used them in jewelry and often offered them to the gods. Today, spiny oyster shells are still valued for their beauty.

Farther inland along the coastal river valleys, the early Andean people **domesticated** many crops that are still enjoyed today. Some forty to fifty rivers cut through the coastal region, and they were eventually used to **irrigate** fields planted with peanuts,

domesticated (duh-MES-ti-kate-id) taken from the wild and tamed to be used by humans

irrigate (IR-uh-gate) to supply water to crops by artificial means, such as channels and pipes

beans, peppers, corn, and sweet potatoes. The river valleys were larger to the north, so people could grow more food there and support larger populations than in the south.

THE ANDEAN HIGHLANDS

The second major region of the Inca Empire was the Andean Highlands. Not far from the coast, the land begins to rise sharply, eventually reaching the high peaks of the Andes, which can soar above 22,000 feet (6,706 m). The region has huge mountain valleys and a variety of climates that allowed the Incas to raise a wide range of domesticated crops. In general, the weather was colder and wetter at the higher peaks, and warmer and drier in the valleys. As in the coastal region, people tended to settle near water, either along rivers, near springs, or close to Lake Titicaca. At an altitude of 12,500 feet (3,810 m), Titicaca is the world's highest navigable lake.

The Incas divided most highland valleys into four main zones by elevation. The first zone was called the *yunga*. It reached up to about 5,000 feet (1,524 m), and irrigation helped the Incas raise

This Inca ceramic statue dates to between 1430 and 1532 CE.

many crops there, such as fruit, vegetables, and cotton. The Incas also raised hundreds of different kinds of tubers at various altitudes.

The coca plant was grown in parts of the yunga. The Incas chewed its leaves because a substance in them makes people alert. Coca was a part of some religious **rites**, too. Indian people of the Andes still use coca. It is also the source of the illegal drug cocaine, and the continued raising and harvesting of coca is a major problem for governments that are trying to stop cocaine use. For many people of Bolivia and Peru, however, coca leaves are a part of their culture that they do not want to abandon.

Lake Titicaca covers about 3,200 square miles (8,288 sq km).

The next zone was the *quechua*, which reached up to about 11,500 feet (3,505 m). Two native crops grown there in Inca times were the grains quinoa and amaranth. Varieties of corn and potatoes also grew at these high altitudes.

The two highest regions in the highlands were the *suni* and *puna*. In the suni, from about 11,500 to 13,000 feet (3,505 to 3,962 m), the Incas could still grow tubers and quinoa. But almost no crops grew in the puna, which was the highest elevation where people lived. Grasses in the high plains, however, were a good food for llamas and alpacas. The Incas raised these **camelids** to use as pack animals. A llama can carry between 50 and 75 pounds (23 and 34 kilograms) on its back for up to 20 miles (32 km) a day.

Llamas and alpacas were also sources of meat and provided wool for clothing. Their bones were turned into tools. Two wild

Coca fields are still a common sight in some parts of the Andes.

camelids (KAM-uh-lidz) animals such as the llama and alpaca that are found in South America and are related to the camel

Corn grew well in the quechua zone.

relatives of these animals are the guanaco and the vicuña. The Incas hunted these wild camelids for meat. At times, they also captured them, shaved off their wool, and then released them back into the wild. People of the Andes still rely on llamas as pack animals and sources of food and wool, and raising llamas has spread to other parts of the world.

THE AMAZON REGION

The eastern slopes of the Andes lead down into what geographers call the Amazon Basin. This third geographic region contains the Amazon River and thousands of square miles of tropical rain forests. The Incas had some colonies in the Amazon region, on the eastern slopes of the Andes. In general, though, their efforts to conquer the lowlands failed. The people of the Amazon lived in small groups, rather than in developed cities, as in the coastal regions and the highlands. If faced with an invasion, the Amazonian residents merely slipped away into the thick forests.

The Incas, though, did have contact with the people of the Amazon region. Some foods the Incas ate, such as peanuts and sweet potatoes, originally came from the eastern side of the Andes. The Incas also traded for prized resources from those lands, such as coca leaves and the colorful feathers of tropical birds, which were used to create clothing for nobles. Jaguars lived in this region, and the Incas greatly respected these animals for their hunting skills and strength. Jaguars often appeared in Inca art, as did monkeys, which also lived in the Amazon region.

The Amazon is the longest river in South America.

Andean peoples used bird feathers to create clothing and other decorative objects.

OTHER NOTABLE WILDLIFE

Soaring above the Inca lands were a variety of large birds, such as hawks, eagles, and condors. The Incas thought they could make predictions about the future by studying the flights of these large birds. The puma, a relative of the jaguar, lived in the highlands and was admired for its hunting ability. The city of Cuzco was said to have been laid out so its buildings and nearby hills formed the shape of this large Andean cat. The condor, the puma, and the snake all played a part in Inca religion. The condor was said to represent the heavens, the puma the earth, and the snake the underworld—the place where the Incas' souls went after a person died.

Another important animal that figured in the daily life of the Inca and other Andean peoples was the guinea pig, known as the *cuy*. Andean people domesticated this rodent and raised it for meat. Guinea pigs were also sacrificed to the gods for some religious ceremonies.

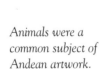

Animals were a common subject of Andean artwork.

CHAPTER FOUR

LIFE IN INCA LANDS

At the height of the Inca Empire, the Sapa Inca ruled over millions of people. Within that population were many distinct groups, separated by social class, wealth, and ethnic and religious backgrounds. Despite living in the Inca Empire, only a few of these millions of people were truly Incas as the rulers saw it. To be an Inca meant having family ties to the legendary first Inca king, Manco Qhapaq, or to the first settlers of Cuzco. But whether they were Incas or members of different ethnic groups, the people had similar family groupings. They believed in the idea of reciprocity in their relationships. And they knew that their positions in life

This hat was likely worn by a member of the elite Inca ruling class.

Inca commoners had little chance for social advancement.

were not likely to change. People born poor commoners usually remained poor commoners for their entire lives, while the Inca rulers controlled politics, trade, and religion.

The Past Is Present
FREEZE-DRYING, THE NATURAL WAY

O ne way to keep certain foods from spoiling is to freeze-dry them. Freeze-drying also makes food weigh less and take up less space, so it is easier to transport and store. Modern freeze-drying methods use complex machinery, but the Incas were freeze-drying food long before such machines were invented. Potatoes, meat, or fish were left out on winter nights to freeze. Then, during the day, they were placed in the sun. The process was repeated until all of the water came out of the foods. Meat preserved this way was called *charqui*, and this word is the source of the modern English word *jerky*, which refers to meat that has been dried to preserve it.

THE RULING INCAS

The true Incas were divided into two groups. The first group, "Incas by blood," traced their roots to Manco Qhapaq and lived in Cuzco. The king and other royals were all members of this group. The men of this group wore large plugs inside stretched earlobe piercings. These plugs indicated their special status, and led to the Spanish nickname, *orejones*, or "big ears." These ruling Incas lived in the center of Cuzco.

The royal Incas belonged to the different panacas, while the nonroyal Incas were grouped together in units called *ayllus*. An ayllu was an extended family or kin group whose members claimed ties to a common ancestor. Ayllus were found in many Andean societies. Members of an ayllu shared land and other resources, and they were expected to look out for one another. Individual families received land to farm based on their size. At times, an ayllu's land was spread out over different elevations. Families were sent to various altitudes to farm different crops, which were shared with the entire ayllu.

The Inca used a series of larger and larger jewelry to stretch holes in their earlobes.

The range of crops and climates helped ensure a steady supply of different foods for everyone.

To help him rule the growing empire, the Inca king Pachakuti was said to have created a second class of people: "Incas by privilege." They belonged to the first tribes the Incas conquered as they moved beyond Cuzco. They had strong loyalty to the ruling Incas and were often sent out as mitmaqs to help settle new lands.

The Incas let most local nobles stay in power as kurakas once they agreed to accept Inca rule. The kurakas formed a social class below the Incas by blood and by privilege. As a member of the ruling class, a kuraka had some special rights. He received servants, did not have to pay taxes, and could ride in a litter. The most loyal kurakas received special gifts from the Incas, such as land, gold, or wives.

THE COMMON PEOPLE

Most of the millions of people who made up the Inca Empire were commoners. They had no political rights, but because the Incas counted on them to raise crops and herd animals, the rulers made sure the common people were generally treated well. In return, the head of each household had to pay a tax, in the form of mit'a. This work could include serving in the army, constructing buildings, or moving goods across the empire. When a family member was away fulfilling the community's tribute obligations, other members of the ayllu helped do his work.

Although most people were farmers, some had special skills, such as metalworking or weaving. Some villages only produced goods such as pottery or clothing for the state. But artisans and their families also worked the fields to raise crops. They did not generally specialize in a single full-time task.

Mining was another important job for some commoners. Inca lands provided gold, silver, copper, and the metals used to make bronze. Only the nobles had silver and gold items, while the commoners had copper and bronze. Taking the metal **ore** out of the earth was hard work, since the only tools the miners had were deer antlers and stones.

Certain common people played special roles in the Inca Empire. *Yanaconas* were people from the provinces chosen by Inca royalty to be their servants. Sometimes the yanaconas were taken from their families at early ages to begin serving. They were often bright and

ore (OR) rock or earth that contains a metal or valuable mineral

Workers mined and panned for gold to provide artisans with materials for their crafts.

highly skilled, and some even served as kurakas. Yanaconas did not have to pay taxes and could pass their positions on to their children.

The Incas picked some beautiful young women, both commoners and Inca royalty, to serve as *aqlla*, or "chosen women." They were taken from their families at a young age and sent to special houses called *aqllawasi*. In the city of Huánuco Pampa, as many as

Inca artisans worked to create beautiful gold jewelry and statues for the nobles.

two hundred of them lived and worked in a separated area that had about fifty buildings. Some aqlla served the gods by taking care of their temples. Others were given as brides to nobles or became the king's secondary wives. A few had musical skills and performed at festivals. In their houses, the aqlla produced high-quality cloth and brewed chicha for redistribution by the Inca state. Some archaeologists have called the aqllas a kind of slave, since they had no freedom to do as they chose. But many within the empire considered it a great honor to have a family member chosen to be an aqlla.

Many modern
descendants of the
Incas continue to spin
wool yarn as their
ancestors did.

Daily Life

The lives of many Andean peoples revolved around their land,
which belonged to their ayllu. In return for their work, the average
subjects of the empires received the food, clothing, and daily items
they needed to survive. The Incas did not have markets where
common people bought and sold goods. In coastal regions and
around Lake Titicaca, water and the resources it provided were
also an important part of life.

In a typical household, a man performed his mit'a work as required, which included going to war to fight for the Sapa Inca. At times, wives went along with their husbands when they fought. At home, men and women farmed, herded camelids, fished, and hunted. They also spun yarn and wove it into clothing. Both men and women took care of the home and raised the children.

The typical Inca home near Cuzco had a rectangular shape with a pointed **thatched** roof. A family lived, ate, and slept in a single room, which had just one door and often no windows. Much of daily life and activity usually took place in the courtyard in front of the house. In some cities, small groups of homes were often located together around a common courtyard, with a wall surrounding the buildings. This compound was called a *kancha*. Some kanchas were built to house government offices or religious sites. Most nobles also lived in one-room homes, though theirs were much larger than those of the commoners. In the provinces, the Incas let conquered people keep their own building styles, which included some round homes or houses with flat roofs made of reeds.

Within such a large empire, a typical daily meal might vary from one location to another. But certain foods were common across the realm. Potatoes and other tubers, corn, quinoa, and chili peppers formed a large part of the diet. Camelids, guinea pigs, and ducks were sources of meat, though meat was consumed much less frequently than vegetables. Along the coast, people caught and ate a variety of fish and shellfish. Food was often prepared as a stew. Chicha was the common drink in the Andes and is still made in parts of Peru. The people of the region also sometimes ate popcorn, as people around the world do today.

thatched (THACHT) made from dried plants, such as straw or reeds

loincloths (LOYN-klawths) garments worn around a man's waist

Inca women often dressed using just two pieces of cloth.

Commoners wore simple clothing. Men in warmer areas wore **loincloths** and shoulder coverings similar to a poncho. In colder areas, they more often wore knee-length tunics. Women wrapped their bodies in a piece of cloth that was held together with a pin. They also wore a separate covering over their shoulders. Many nobles wore clothing with bright colors or fancy designs. Everyone wore sandals.

The government tightly controlled the making of cloth and which clothes were worn by certain groups. People from different ethnic groups wore different styles of clothing. This made it easy to identify members of different groups. Hats were one common indicator of a person's home region. Mitmaqs would not be able to leave the land they had been assigned to, since their clothing would call attention to them if they went to a different place. Cotton and wool were the most common yarns used to make clothes. The best cloth, made of the finest wool fibers, was called *cumbi*. It was often burned as a sacrifice to the gods.

GROWING UP INCA

The Incas did not mark the birth of their children with any special celebrations. After giving birth, a mother washed her baby and then went back to work, carrying

the child on her back. Children were not named until after they were one year old—perhaps because so many children died as infants. The naming ceremony included the child's first haircut.

Most Inca children did not go to school. They learned the skills they would need as adults from their parents. Only the girls chosen to be aqllas and the sons of Inca nobility and conquered rulers received a formal education. The boys attended a school in Cuzco where they learned Quechua. They also learned religious teachings, history, and how to use khipus.

Like their ancestors, contemporary Andean people wear a variety of colorful hats.

Animal sacrifices were a part of many Inca ceremonies.

Inca boys were considered men once they were about fourteen years old. A special ceremony was held when a boy became a man. The ceremony included dancing and the sacrifice of a lamb. Girls went through their own ceremonies at around the same age. Relatives gave a feast and gave the girls gifts. Young women were often married a few years after becoming adults, while men waited until they were in their mid-twenties. For commoners, the state had to approve a man's choice of a bride. A husband and wife had to come from the same ayllu, though they could not be closely related. Noblemen could have more than one wife, though historians are not sure how many nobles engaged in this practice.

As depicted in this European illustration, royal Incas were only allowed to marry other royals.

CHAPTER FIVE

A RELIGIOUS CULTURE

On a high Andean peak, Inca priests led three children to a special platform on the summit of a mountain more than 22,000 feet (6,706 m) in elevation. Dressed in their finest

Archaeologists have discovered the bodies of sacrificed Inca children.

clothes, the children had traveled some 500 miles (805 km) to reach this mountain in what is now Argentina. Between the travel, the chicha they drank, and the effects of the high altitude on their bodies, the children began to weaken. They lay down, and the priests killed them, either by hitting them on the head or strangling them.

The mummies of these three children were found in 1999. The freezing temperatures at the mountaintop had preserved their bodies. The Incas believed that mountains were powerful spirits called *apus* and that people would have better contact with the gods at a mountain's peak. The children who died on this mountain were sacrifices. The Incas believed that after their deaths, the children would send messages from the gods back to earth, through their religious leaders.

Sacrifices were often made to win the gods' favor. Items such as food, clothing, gold and silver artwork, animals, and even humans were given as offerings. Children were often chosen because they were thought of as pure—they had not had much time to do evil things.

The Incas sometimes made offerings of chicha to the sun god.

The Past Is Present
THE MOTHER SEED

Quinoa was an important crop for the Incas and other Andean people. This nutritious food could grow at high altitudes and was a good source of protein. The Incas called it the "mother seed," and it is actually the seed of a plant related to spinach, rather than a true grain. Quinoa has sometimes been called a lost food, since the Spanish largely ignored it after their conquest, and its use did not spread beyond the Andes. But in recent years, quinoa has

become popular around the world. That demand has raised prices for quinoa grown in its Andean homeland, which is good news for Bolivian farmers. But the higher price is bad for the poor people of the region, who are finding it harder to buy this key part of their diet. In 2011, Bolivian officials reported that many children were suffering from poor nutrition because they were eating less quinoa.

Human sacrifice was fairly common in the Andes for several thousand years before the rise of the Incas. This practice might seem cruel or shocking today, but it made sense to Andean peoples, in their view of the world and of the gods that created and watched over it. The gods had to be thanked for their efforts to help humans, or given gifts to ensure that they would help in the future. This tied in with the Inca belief in reciprocity. For the Incas, religion and the gods were an important part of daily life.

THE INCA GODS

The Inca origin stories held that Wiraqocha was the creator of the universe, and the first Incas were his children. But the sun god Inti had the most direct influence on Inca leaders, since the sun was essential for all forms of life. The temple Qorikancha in Cuzco, dedicated to Inti, was the Incas' most important religious site. Its

The sun was a central figure in Inca religion.

name means "enclosure of gold," and the Spanish marveled at the wealth they saw there when they first stormed it. The Inca king was considered to be a human form of Inti and his son, and the worship of the sun god was the official state religion. But the Incas believed that many other gods shaped the natural world and the events of human lives.

Radiating out from Inti's temple were invisible lines the Incas called *ceques*. Along these lines were the most important *wakas*, or **shrines**, of the Inca religion. Some of the more than three hundred wakas along the ceques mark places where important mythical events occurred. Others were sources of water or other sacred natural sites.

Ceque lines spread from a central point at Inti's temple in Cuzco.

Different kinds of wakas located along the ceque lines included springs, carved stones, and caves. The Incas believed that wakas contained powerful spirits.

In addition to Wiracocha and Inti, other important Inca gods included Illapa, the god of thunder and lightning; the moon goddess Mama Quilla; Mama Cocha, the source of all water on Earth; and Pachamama, who was Earth herself. These and other gods had their own places of worship, where priests held ceremonies to honor them. The Incas did not force the people they defeated to worship Inca gods. Local religions remained in place. But the Incas did take holy objects from the foreigners and kept them in Cuzco. If a defeated people refused to obey Inca rule, the Incas would punish the rebellious nation by harming its sacred objects.

RELIGIOUS RITES AND CEREMONIES

The Incas believed that some people could communicate with the gods. Some religious events were centered on the oracles who spoke with the gods and interpreted their holy messages. Each year, the high priest associated with Inti held a meeting in Cuzco with other important oracles from across the empire. The king wanted to know what the gods had in store. Oracles who made favorable predictions that came true received gifts from the king. But predictions that did not come true or were negative upset some kings. Atawallpa became angry when one oracle predicted that he would not fare well in the civil war with his brother Waskar. The enraged Atawallpa is said to have beheaded the oracle with a battle-ax in response.

One important religious rite was mummification. To the Incas, a dead and mummified ancestor was a link between the gods and the living. Only the most important family members became

This carving of a human head may have been buried along with an Inca mummy.

mummies, but those who did were treated well by the living. Relatives brought the dead food, clothing, and other gifts. The mummies of dead kings were treated especially well.

MEASURING AND COUNTING

Recording the passing of time, by days and months, had religious importance for the Incas. The Inca calendar was used to keep track of when certain religious ceremonies were held. The Incas actually had two calendars. One was based on the cycle of the moon, and the other was based on the daily movement of the sun. The first had only about 354 days, so the Incas sometimes had to add days to a month so the calendar would agree with the 365-day year based on the sun.

The Incas tracked the movement of the sun and stars through the sky. Stone towers in Cuzco lined up with the position of the sun as it rose and set on the longest and shortest days of the year.

The calendar was also important for telling the Incas when to perform certain farming tasks. February and March were the time for harvesting some potatoes and other tubers. In May, the first corn was harvested. By November, the Incas would begin to irrigate their fields for the next crop of corn, which they had planted in September.

Measuring distance and area was important for the Incas' many building projects. Engineers had to know how big certain stones should be. Some units of measurement seem to have been based on the human body—the size of a palm or the height of a typical man. A standard measure of area was the *topo*, which was a rectangle 300 x 150 feet (91 x 46 m).

For counting, the Incas used a specially made tray that could hold pebbles, which were assigned different values. As most people do today, the Incas used a decimal system—a number system based on units of ten.

Many examples of the Incas' masterful architecture still stand.

ARCHITECTURE

Architecture played an important role in Inca religion. Where cities were built or how the buildings were placed often tied in to religious beliefs about what made a spot sacred. Some of the most impressive examples of Inca architecture are temples. The Qorikancha has been called the most sacred building in the empire. Today, its walls still stand beneath a church the Spanish built on top of it. The stones used to build the many important

These expertly carved stones hold together without needing any sort of mortar or cement.

structures in Cuzco and elsewhere throughout the empire show the Incas' great engineering skills. The stones fit so tightly together that a knife blade cannot be slipped in between them. The Incas did not use cement or any other substance to hold the stones together. They were carved and shaped to fit together perfectly. Some lesser buildings, however, did have walls that used a type of mud to hold the stones together.

Inca buildings had several distinct features. Doorways were usually shaped as trapezoids—rectangles with two parallel sides—so the sides angled in as they went up. Important buildings also had double jambs, or a second, inner doorway that was smaller than the one right in front of it.

Roads were another example of the Incas' building skills. At times, Inca builders tunneled roads through solid rock. A road might be paved with stones in rainy areas. In dry regions, the road was simply a dirt path lined by a low wall of stones or adobe blocks. In some places, wooden and stone markers showed a road's path. In others, walls kept travelers from the farms located near the road. Bridges made of rope spanned rivers, sometimes covering more than 150 feet (46 m).

The Incas used their swinging rope bridges to forge paths throughout the Andes.

Textile makers wove colorful geometric patterns into cloth.

SKILLED ARTISANS AND ARTISTS

Skilled Inca artisans created both beautiful art objects and useful items. Metalworkers from Chimú were prized for their talents in working with silver and gold. Silver was associated with the moon and gold with the sun. Small gold and silver figures of people and animals were sometimes buried with the dead. Bronze, which was made from tin, was used to make everyday items, such as axes and knives. Perhaps most important of all were the textile makers, who created the materials used for clothing.

Most of the items made for daily use, such as pottery and clothing, had elements of design and color. So did cups called *keros*, which could be made of wood, metal, or pottery. The Sapa Inca gave away pairs of these cups to rival leaders to seek their friendship.

Music and singing were an important part of Inca culture. Inca musicians learned to play flutes and panpipes. A panpipe consists of several pieces of cane tied together. The pieces are of different lengths, so blowing into each one produces a different note. Andean musicians still play panpipes and can be found in cities around the world playing their native music on the streets. Other Inca instruments included drums, rattles, and conch shells, which were played as trumpets. Dancing to the music was limited to festivals and religious events.

Inca songs were usually poems that were set to music. The poems often dealt with Inca history and the gods. The songs and poems were important for spreading Inca culture, since the Incas did not have books.

Flutes were sometimes made from bones that were carefully carved with decorations.

CHAPTER SIX

THE END OF THE EMPIRE

I n 1532, his battle against his brother Waskar over, Atawallpa
and his victorious army traveled to Cuzco. Along the way, they
heard about Spaniards who had landed on the north coast of

Francisco Pizarro led expeditions to South America in search of wealth and glory.

Peru. The Inca ruler sent the foreign strangers gifts, such as servants and food. The leader of the Spaniards, Francisco Pizarro, sent the new emperor several gifts in return.

In November, the Spaniards met with Atawallpa in the town of Cajamarca. With Atawallpa were thousands of Inca soldiers. Pizarro commanded about 160 troops, fewer than half of whom were on horseback. The Spaniards made camp in Cajamarca, and Pizarro began making plans for a daring attack that would change world history.

Advanced weapons such as the harquebus allowed the Spanish to get the upper hand over the Incas.

CAPTURING A KING

Although badly outnumbered, Pizarro and his men had better weapons than the Incas had, including a form of gun called a harquebus. They also had much stronger armor, and they counted on the element of surprise. The Spaniards hid behind buildings in the main plaza of Cajamarca and waited for Atawallpa to arrive. He came with about two thousand men to meet Pizarro. The gold and silver they wore amazed the Spaniards. As the soldiers waited for the signal to attack, a Spanish priest approached Atawallpa. He told the king that the Incas should give up their gods, become

The capture of Atawallpa struck a major blow to the Incas.

Christians, and obey the king of Spain. Atawallpa took a book the priest held, then threw it to the ground. With that, the hiding Spaniards poured into the plaza, firing their harquebuses and small cannons.

In the fighting that followed, the Incas seemed to barely fight back. By some accounts, most of them were unarmed. The Incas were stunned by the enemy's tactics. Several hundred died, and many others were wounded. The Spaniards then kidnapped Atawallpa and imprisoned him in the main temple of Cajamarca.

Though a prisoner, Atawallpa could still receive guests, and he often met with Pizarro. Atawallpa began to see how much the Spaniards valued gold, and he made Pizarro an offer. He would give the Spaniards a roomful of gold and silver if they released him. Pizarro agreed, and some of Atawallpa's men traveled to Cuzco to retrieve the king's riches. The Spaniards melted these great works of Inca art into bars of gold and silver. Once the ransom reached Pizarro, he had the king killed.

The Past Is Present
CULTIVATING ANCIENT CROPS

The potato is the world's best-known Peruvian crop. Other tubers eaten in Inca times, such as the *oca* and *ulluco*, are still important parts of Andean meals. The International Potato Center (CIP), an organization based in Lima, studies the many different types of potatoes and tubers that the Incas counted on for a large part of their diet, some of which are now extremely rare. Research at the CIP helps native farmers produce more of these important crops by saving seeds of rapidly disappearing native plants.

Recent work at the CIP has looked at *maca*, one of the Andean tubers. The crop can grow at altitudes above 13,000 feet (3,962 m). Inca warriors ate maca, which is packed with nutrients, as they marched across the empire. Maca also contains chemicals with medical benefits, and more Peruvian farmers are now returning to its cultivation. Scientists at the CIP are also working with farmers to preserve other ancient Inca tubers, such as oca, *yacon*, and *arracacha*.

Ruling the Empire

Pizarro wanted more than the Incas' gold. He wanted to claim the empire as part of Spain. To rule a colony so far from Europe, Spain would need a loyal local ruler in charge. The Spaniards named Manco Inca the new king, but he was actually under Spanish control. Manco Inca was another son of Wayna Qhapaq. He ruled for several years, but soon tired of the way the Spanish treated him and his people. In 1536, he fled Cuzco and led a rebellion. Fighting raged in Cuzco and in the city of Lima, which the Spanish had recently established on the coast. The Spanish successfully defended Lima, and the fighting at Cuzco ended when many of the Incas left the battlefield to tend their crops.

With the Spanish back in control, they brought in a new Inca king, Paullu Inca, to serve their interests. The Inca lands became the heart of a colony that Spain called Peru. Meanwhile, Manco Inca's family tried to keep alive a separate, independent Inca state based in Vilcabamba.

Inca rulers claimed the title of Sapa Inca until 1572. That year, a Spanish force

Atawallpa made good on his promise to deliver a room full of gold.

marched on Vilcabamba and captured the last Inca king, Tupac Amaru. He was taken to Cuzco and executed, marking the end of Inca resistance to Spanish rule.

Despite the rebels based in Vilcabamba, a growing number of Incas came to accept Spanish rule. The Spanish crown won the support of Inca nobles and kurakas by giving them land and a role to play in governing the large class of commoners. These nobles also did not have to pay tribute to the Spanish. Still, the arrival of the Spanish meant many changes for the Incas and others who had direct contact with them. To name one, the new government did not believe in reciprocity. The colony existed only to serve the interests of the Spanish king and his subjects in Peru.

Manco Inca was unsuccessful in his attempts to drive the Spanish from Cuzco.

Some Incas continued to fight against the Spanish for many years.

Meanwhile, the Spanish conquistadores instituted an *encomienda* system. They were not landowners, but they received a portion of the crops or goods that the local people produced. Over time, the Spanish increased the amount of tribute they expected from the encomienda workers. If they could not produce it, the locals were forced to sell the land to the Spanish. A large class of landless people developed, and many were forced to work as servants for the Spanish. As part of the encomienda system, the Spaniards also enslaved the local peoples and forced them to construct buildings and make clothing. Later, many of the defeated peoples were made to work in the gold and silver mines. To enforce their rule, the Spanish sometimes turned to violence.

In remote areas, the local people mostly lived as they had before. But some were forced to move to new towns built by the Spanish. They also began to raise crops and animals that the Spanish settlers brought from Europe, such as wheat and cattle. At the same time, they grew the corn and quinoa they always ate. Over time, though, as the Spanish demanded more European foods as tribute, the Incas could not grow as much of their own food.

The Spanish introduced their Roman Catholic religion to the Incas. The process of converting the people was slow, because in the early years of the colony, few Catholic priests reached Peru. The priests who did arrive made a point of destroying mummies and any other sacred objects they could find. The royal mummies were early targets, and as a result, archaeologists have never found the mummy of an Inca king. Despite the priests' efforts, people in some small towns secretly kept alive some traditional religious beliefs and practices, and many of these survive in the Andes today.

The Spanish treated the conquered Incas with great cruelty.

93

THE LASTING INCA INFLUENCE

The Spanish introduced the Inca to foods and animals such as horses and cattle, while in turn learning about new foods and animals from the Inca. The Spanish brought some of these foods back to Spain, where they spread across Europe and to other Spanish colonies. These foods included corn, potatoes, and chili peppers.

The Incas' domesticated animals are also found in many parts of the world today. Guinea pigs are popular pets, and llamas are still sometimes used as pack animals. Vicuña, the source of the finest wool for the Inca nobility, is still prized for its warmth and softness. People of the Andes still take part in *chacus*—the herding of vicuñas into areas where their wool can be clipped before they are returned to the wild. The rarity of the wool makes it expensive, providing a good source of income for descendants of the Incas.

Those descendants are perhaps the most direct tie between the modern Andean nations and the Incas. Between thirteen million and sixteen million people speak Quechua, the language of the ancient empire. It is one of the official languages of Peru and Bolivia. Some Quechua words have made their way into English, through Spanish. The condor, a huge bird found in parts of the Western Hemisphere, was known as *kuntur* in Quechua.

Many of today's Quechua speakers live as the commoners of the Inca Empire did. Some still use foot plows, simple tools used to prepare the soil for planting. Some still chew coca leaves for a quick boost of energy. Worship of the traditional gods continues in some areas, even after the Roman Catholic Church came to dominate religion in the region. Some people still farm land on terraces built by the Incas.

In Peru, Ecuador, and Bolivia, the heart of the old Inca Empire, people sometimes choose names that refer to the past.

Some modern Andeans dress in the traditional clothing of their ancestors during chacus.

Andean weavers continue to create cloth using traditional materials and patterns.

Tupac Amaru was the last Inca king, and modern-day rebels in Peru chose his name for the name of their group. A popular American rapper, Tupac Shakur, also named himself for the Inca ruler. Across the Andes, arts groups and organizations that promote the region's culture often include the word *Inca* (or *Inka*) in their names.

The movement of people out of Peru and Bolivia has helped spread some lasting influences. Two Ecuadorian-Americans formed the musical group Inka Gold, which uses traditional reed pipes as well as modern instruments. There is even a soft drink that is known as Inca Kola, and a version of it is sold in parts of North America.

Parts of today's Andean culture have roots that go back much farther than Inca times. The people of Cuzco who called themselves Incas and built an empire drew on many

Inca culture continues to influence our world today.

other civilizations. But the Incas, with their political and military skill, built the South American empire that most people know of today. Their contact with the Spanish conquistadores linked the cultures of many lands in an enduring way.

BIOGRAPHIES

ATAWALLPA (CA. 1502–1533) was a son of Wayna Qhapaq who battled his brother Waskar for control of the empire after their father's death. Atawallpa won, but he was killed by the Spanish before he ever reached Cuzco to rule.

BERNABÉ COBO (1582–1657) was a Spanish priest who spent time in Peru and wrote one of the most respected secondary accounts of Inca history and culture.

MANCO INCA (CA. 1516–1544) was chosen by the Spanish to rule the Incas. Manco Inca rebelled twice against them. He set up a separate Inca state in Vilcabamba, which his sons ruled for several decades.

PACHAKUTI (?–1471) was the Inca king who is said to have founded the Inca Empire and turned Cuzco into a great city. He also built the royal estate at Machu Picchu, the most famous Inca ruins.

FRANCISCO PIZARRO (CA. 1475–1541) was the Spanish conquistador who defeated the Incas and seized the empire for Spain. A battle between rival groups of Spaniards for control of Peru led to his death.

TOPA INCA (?–1493) was the son of Pachakuti. Through his conquests, Topa Inca expanded Inca control south into what became Chile and Argentina and north into what became Ecuador.

TUPAC AMARU (?–1572) was the last of Manco Inca's sons to rule in Vilcabamba. He was captured and killed by the Spanish.

WASKAR (?–1532) claimed the title of Sapa Inca after the death of his father, Wayna Qhapaq, but his brother Atawallpa challenged him for the throne and won.

WAYNA QHAPAQ (?–CA. 1525) was the great leader whose conquests as Sapa Inca extended Inca influence to the northernmost highlands and the coast of Ecuador. He ruled when the Spanish first reached Inca lands.

TIMELINE

CA. 1100: *End of Wari and Tiwanaku influence in the Cuzco valley*

500	1000	1100	1200

CA. 600 CE: *People from Wari begin to settle near Cuzco.*

1438: *Pachakuti's reign begins (traditional date for the founding of the Inca Empire).*

1471: *Pachakuti gives control of the empire to Topa Inca, who greatly expands its borders.*

1532: *Atawallpa wins the civil war; he meets Francisco Pizarro, who kidnaps him.*

1300   **1400**   **1500**   **1525**

CA. **1463:** *Pachakuti begins to share power with his son Topa Inca.*

CA. **1525:** *Wayna Qhapaq receives the first reports of Spaniards in the empire; he dies soon after, marking the start of a civil war between his sons, Atawallpa and Waskar.*

CA. **1300:** *Inca control begins to spread through the valley.*

(timeline continued)

1536: Manco Inca leads a rebellion against the Spanish.

1537: The Spanish end the rebellion, and Manco Inca flees to Vilcabamba.

1538: Manco Inca launches another rebellion, which also fails.

1550   1575   1600

1533: Pizarro executes Atawallpa.

1572: The Spanish kill the last Inca king, Tupac Amaru.

1911: Hiram Bingham of Yale University discovers Machu Picchu and later introduces its wonders to the world.

1944: Peru introduces a modern version of the Inti Raymi, an Inca festival honoring the sun god.

| 1700 | 1800 | 1900 | 2000 |

2011: Yale University returns Inca artifacts to the Peruvian government.

GLOSSARY

ancestors (AN-ses-turz) relatives who lived long ago

archaeology (ar-kee-AH-luh-jee) the study of the distant past, which often involves digging up old buildings, objects, and bones and examining them carefully

artisans (AHR-ti-zuhnz) people who are skilled at working with their hands at a particular craft

camelids (KAM-uh-lidz) animals such as the llama and alpaca that are found in South America and are related to the camel

campaigns (kam-PAYNZ) organized actions in order to achieve a particular goal

conquistadores (kahn-KEES-tuh-dohrz) soldiers sent to seize foreign lands for Spain

coronation (kor-uh-NAY-shun) the ceremony in which a king, queen, or other ruler is crowned

current (KUR-uhnt) the movement of water in a definite direction in a river or an ocean

domesticated (duh-MES-ti-kate-id) taken from the wild and tamed to be used by humans

famine (FAM-in) a serious lack of food in a geographic area

irrigate (IR-uh-gate) to supply water to crops by artificial means, such as channels and pipes

judicial (joo-DISH-uhl) having to do with a court of law or a judge

litter (LIT-ur) a covered couch or seat that is carried by several people

loincloths (LOYN-klawths) garments worn around a man's waist

mummy (MUHM-ee) a dead body that has been preserved with special chemicals and wrapped in cloth

oracles (OR-uh-kulz) people who are thought to be in touch with gods and spirits and can predict the future; also, the places where those people deliver their messages from the gods

ore (OR) rock or earth that contains a metal or valuable mineral

reciprocity (reh-si-PRAH-si-tee) an arrangement between two people or groups in which each owes something to or does something for the other

rites (RITES) religious events or activities with special meaning

sacrificed (SAK-ruh-fyst) killed as an offering to a god

shrines (SHRINZ) buildings or locations connected to a religious figure or event

subjects (SUHB-jekts) people who live under the authority of a king or queen

thatched (THACHT) made from dried plants, such as straw or reeds

tribute (TRIB-yoot) something done, given, or said to show thanks or respect, or to repay an obligation

Western Hemisphere (WES-turn HEM-i-sfeer) the half of the world that includes North and South America and the waters around these two continents

FIND OUT MORE

BOOKS

Gruber, Beth. *Ancient Inca: Archaeology Unlocks the Secrets of the Inca's Past.* Washington, DC: National Geographic, 2007.

Hunefeldt, Christine. *A Brief History of Peru.* New York: Facts on File, 2010.

Kops, Deborah. *Machu Picchu.* Minneapolis: Twenty-First Century Books, 2009.

Roza, Greg. *Incan Mythology and Other Myths of the Andes.* New York: Rosen Publishing Group, 2008.

Sonneborn, Liz. *Pizarro: Conqueror of the Mighty Incas.* Berkeley Heights, NJ: Enslow Publishers, 2010.

Visit this Scholastic Web site for more information on Ancient Incas:
www.factsfornow.scholastic.com
Enter the keywords **Ancient Incas**

INDEX

Page numbers in *italics* indicate a photograph or map.

ABOUT THE AUTHOR

Michael Burgan is the author of more than 250 books for children and young adults, both fiction and nonfiction. His works include books on the Roman, Mongol, and Persian Empires and biographies of U.S. leaders. His graphic-novel adaptation of *Frankenstein* was a Junior Library Guild selection. A graduate of the University of Connecticut with a degree in history, Burgan is also a produced playwright. He lives in Santa Fe, New Mexico.